Alligators

and *Music*

Published by G A M B I T

of Meeting House Green in Ipswich Massachusetts

Alligators
and Music

BY DONALD ELLIOTT

and illustrated by

CLINTON ARROWOOD

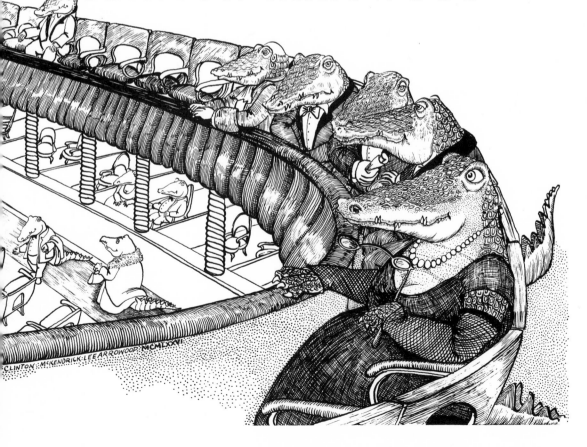

Third Printing

DEDICATION

This book is dedicated to musical alligators; no, to musical instruments; no, to musicians; no . . . to music itself, that divine spark which can elevate musicians, their instruments, and even alligators to dizzy, wonderful heights.

Contents

A Brief Foreword

This is a book designed primarily to be entertaining. Music and art are, after all — or perhaps before all — meant to be entertaining in the best sense of the word, and while it is obvious that they can be and, indeed, are, highly complex, their basic raison d'être must, finally, be concerned with providing enjoyment and esthetic pleasure. But in addition to these values, listening to music and looking at art can also be experiences leading subtly and indirectly to knowledge, if not wisdom, and such a development can be considered as a happy concomitant which often comes naturally and without conscious effort.

Alligators and Music strives to follow these ideas by presenting drawings of musical instruments and short descriptive passages that are not only somewhat whimsically entertaining but that are also educational, for the instruments are reproduced with accuracy and the text attempts to give some indication of the function, sound and relative importance of the fundamental instruments of the orchestra. Although what the instruments say is not always to be taken completely seriously, the point, nonetheless, is to acquaint the reader of any age with them, to give him a bit of a notion of what they are and what they can do — individually as well as in their roles as parts of a larger whole — and to accomplish these objectives in such a way that he enjoys the process. Done successfully, a similar undertaking in almost any field produces something which both teaches *and* gives pleasure, and it could perhaps be hoped that all education would follow such a pattern.

If one is interested in exploring details of the composition of a symphony orchestra or of the characteristics of individual instruments, there are many admirable texts available that will provide any degree of detail desired. But the concern here is only with the general concept of the orchestra and only with its basic instruments. In most cases these instruments fall into four categories — string, woodwind, brass, and percussion — and the drawings and text for some twenty or so of them have been arranged to follow this categorization, although a few instruments that do not seem to fit neatly into specific groups have also been included. As a sort of finale, the entire orchestra is presented, together with the suggestion that regardless of the diverse qualities and values of the separate instruments, the orchestra is a whole, and that while it is composed of many parts, it is considerably more than merely the sum of these parts. Rather obviously, some familiarity with music and musical instruments will make the book more enjoyable to anyone, but if such familiarity does not already exist, perhaps *Alligators and Music* will produce it before the first visit to a live symphony concert.

One of the many unique characteristics of music and art is that they are appealing and accessible on many levels. The child can often enjoy them on his childlike level (which may not, by the way, always be a completely simple one) and the adult can enjoy them on his level, possibly seeing in them certain subtleties, nuances, and abstractions that are essentially beyond the child. It is hoped that this volume, in a similar way, will appeal to a number of levels of feeling and understanding, and that the adult will find in it things as pleasurable — although different — as those which, presumably, the child will find.

It would, therefore, be a bit inaccurate to say that this is a book solely or even primarily "for children." Rather, it represents an attempt to speak to the childlike quality which, although so often sadly repressed in our obsession with maturity, nevertheless remains in all of us in at least a vestigial sense. This is the quality of uncomplicated feeling, of delight in simple things, and of a non-analytical response to those things. This book, then, *is* for children, but it is also for anyone who can temper his maturity with a certain childlike grace.

There remains one final point to consider. The question could be asked, "Why alligators?" The most immediate answer that springs to mind is, "Why *not* alligators?" Perhaps some children will be able to supply better answers.

D. E. AND C. A.

OF ALLIGATORS & MUSIC

Do you know what a symphony orchestra is? Do you know that it is made up of dozens of different musical instruments — some strings, some woodwinds, some brasses, some percussion, and some that do not fall easily into any particular group — and that each instrument has a character of its own? Whether you do or not, maybe you would like to hear what some of them have to say about themselves. If so, just turn the page, look, and listen.

PART I

The Individual Instruments

THE STRING FAMILY

We are the strings. Long or short, heavy or light, we are the heart of the orchestra. When we are set in motion, we make the melodies, and we can be loud or we can be soft, or we can be fast and airy or as slow and deep as the ocean. We do it all, and here we are.

The Violin

The whole orchestra is only a background for me. It sets me up, it prepares the way for me, and when I play with all my fellows, then everyone can see what an orchestra really is! I play the melodies, I produce MUSIC, I am what it's all about. Vibrating strings — that is what I am — and when the bow is drawn over them and the violinist's fingers flash up and down my neck, the melodies that spill forth will break your heart or stir your blood. And although I contribute so much, I demand much, too, for if I am not handled perfectly, I will scratch and screech, and that is not what I was meant to do! Sometimes I wonder why the other instruments are needed at all. Why aren't most symphonies composed for violins alone? Now there's a thought! But is it possible that I am wrong, that the others really are necessary? Preposterous! I could do it all myself — I think.

"I could do it all myself – I think."

The Viola

It's not true, of course, that violins become violas when they grow up, but I must admit it would be good if it were true, because they could do with a little growing up, I think. But considering everything, they aren't really such bad sorts; it's not their fault they don't have the ability to be quite as rich and mellow and full of tone as I am. For although I am just a bit larger in size than the violins, I feel much larger in spirit. But I certainly don't want to let them know that I am superior; after all, we should look at *everyone* as a brother, and I do feel particularly close, in a big-brotherly sort of way, to the violins, although I can't help being just a little irritated sometimes when I see that they get to play most of the best melodies. But no matter; it is good to be kind and generous to little brothers.

"I certainly don't want to let them know
that I am superior."

The 'Cello

I'm so grateful to be a string instrument that doesn't need to be blown upon or struck, and I'm particularly grateful that I am neither one of those tiny, high-pitched violins nor one of those huge, double basses. My sounds, like my size, are right in between, not frivolous and not ridiculously serious, but warm, full, and — well — just right. The rich and elegant wood in my body generates incredibly marvelous and expressive sounds at the merest touch of the bow to my strings, and I don't dominate everyone else the way some of those brasses try to do. I'm glad, too, that I'm so modest despite all the beauty I bring into existence.

"I'm glad, too, that I'm so modest . . ."

The Double Bass

Those violins! They think they're so important! It's just because there are so many of them! They do go along at a great rate, don't they? But when I come along, no one pays too much attention to them anymore. Because when the bow is drawn over my long strings, the sounds that come forth are deep and round and — yes — serious, too. I *can* play melodies, but more often I produce an important sort of deep thrumming vibration, something like a heartbeat, and maybe just as important for the orchestra. I suppose we couldn't really do without those violins, and they are, after all, part of the string family, but when it comes to something serious and important, you can be sure the responsibility will be mine. I can't understand why everyone doesn't realize that.

"Those violins! They think they're so important!"

THE WOODWIND FAMILY

We are the woodwinds, vibrating columns of air, long columns and short columns. We are mellow or shrill, or soft as a whisper. We combine the mysterious with the clear, the dark with the light, and here we are.

The Flute

There is nothing so important as purity — purity of soul, purity of feeling. And how can one be pure unless he is made, as I am, of the finest of woods, or of gold or silver or platinum? It may be true that some people don't always consider me quite as important as some of the other instruments, but that's because I don't really care to overwhelm everything else. That wouldn't be pure. I am completely content to make the kind of music for which I was created, and although it always consists just of single notes, one at a time, it can be a cascade of them, up and down the scale and always clear and pure. If I am heard and appreciated, that's fine, but it isn't necessary. To be pure, one must be concerned not with what people think but with what one is. And I am pure.

"There is nothing so important as purity."

The Oboe

I wonder, often, why I feel so mournful. The sounds I produce make me sad. Music makes me sad. In fact, *everything* seems to make me sad. I think of loneliness and of things gone by that will never come again, of people who have lost their friends, and of the last leaves of autumn. But, somehow, there is a kind of soft joy in this, because I see a gentle sort of beauty in loneliness and a sad kind of happiness in remembering yesterday.

So maybe I am not really mournful. Maybe it is just that I cannot be as bright and lively as some of the other instruments and that I prefer to show through my gentle tones that the loveliest music can also have a hint of sadness in it. After all, it would be a little boring always to be cheerful and light and happy, wouldn't it?

à Basil Reeve

"I wonder, often, why I feel so mournful."

The Clarinet

I wish I could describe to you in words what contentment really means. It has something to do with what one does, but probably more with being *happy* with what one does. It has something to do with dreaming a bit, with being open and communicative but also with holding back something, with dreaming dreams that can never be completely communicated.

Perhaps if you listen to me you will be able to understand what I mean. Listen to how clear and singing my sounds are, how relaxed, cool, liquid, and sometimes mysterious they are, how agile I am, but listen also for something more, the something which breathes softly, "I am what I am, and I am glad to be what I am."

Do you see it? You may, if you listen well, but I think it may be much easier if you can come to the same feeling within yourself!

à Mr Ignatius Gennusa

"I wish I could describe . . . what contentment really means."

The Bassoon

If *you* had a name like "bassoon," how do you think you would sound? Would your tones be light and tinkly, or sweet and sticky, or maybe just harsh and noisy? Certainly not! To be a bassoon they would have to be round and hollow and mellow. They would have to be full of feeling and serious, but not *too* serious, light and quick enough to play lively melodies and to laugh, but also heavy enough to be heard, to be solid, to make an impression. I know, because I *am* a bassoon, and I know the wide range of sounds of which I am capable.

But I have another question for you: do you think I make bassoonlike sounds because I *am* a bassoon, or do you think I am a bassoon because I make bassoonlike sounds? Perhaps I should tell you that I am something of a deep thinker, too, besides being a maker of music.

". . . I am something of a deep thinker . . ."

THE BRASS FAMILY

We are the brasses, solid as the metals from which we are made. We can shout or we can mumble, but whatever we do, you can be sure that there will be no mistake as to who we are. We don't care so much for suggestions; we make statements, and here we are.

The Trumpet

Let us avoid sentimentality and imagination and talk about what is real. Let us not pretend; let us always say things directly. Let us be clear and straightforward and loud enough to be heard. Let us not be afraid to say what should be said, to let people know that they have *really* heard, not just imagined that they have heard.

I am made of brass, the powerful metal, and I will always be strong when the breath of life flows through me like a great and sweeping wind. It is not just a single sound that bursts from me — one which could wake the dead — but often many, a whole string of them to clear the air. I cannot be ignored, for my call is clear, direct, and unmistakable. It is not a matter of chance that God gave his angels horns and that when Gabriel is finally ready it is I who will be summoned to perform!

"I cannot be ignored!"

The French Horn

I come from a long line of horns going back to the days when horsemen hunted through the woods and fields, blowing their horns as they chased the wily fox or the bounding deer. I have a clear and golden sound, a little like nature itself, and while I can be mysterious and soft at times, I can also be majestic and noble. I know what you want to ask, though: why must I have all those curvy tubes like noodles on a dish? I *need* them, that's why, to produce my music, and I'm proud to be so complicated. Life isn't simple, you know, and if you want to make a real contribution to it, you must do and be many things. Do you want to know why a lady is playing me in the picture? I'm not going to tell you; I have to keep *some* secrets to myself!

". . . I'm proud to be so complicated!"

The Trombone

Whenever a group or society of any sort is formed, distinctions among members must be expected. Some members will be, I'm afraid, just a little more common, a little more ordinary, a little less capable than others. Those of us in the upper levels of excellence are obviously more aristocratic and more noble than others, and I, the noble trombone, occupy a position of grandeur and superiority that is very clearly right and proper for me. I am capable, of course, of brilliant and glorious sound, but I can also be mournful, threatening, and profound, and I graciously accept the majestic position my nature has given me. Greatness, too, as everyone knows, is associated with uncomplicated strength; my tones are varied by a simple and noble slide, a mechanism requiring no petty complexities like valves or strings or reeds. I do dislike having to state *all* my virtues, but I think I should also at least mention that I *am* unusually handsome.

It is sometimes, of course, a trifle lonely at the top, but that is one of the prices, I suppose, which one pays when he is as noble as I am. The only thing that bothers and irritates me a little is that I am not completely certain whether all the other instruments realize just how noble I really am. Something ought to be done with those in any group who don't know their betters! What's that? You say there may be some who are better than I? What nonsense! Someone as noble as I shouldn't have to be bothered by having such nagging little thoughts brought up.

". . . I, the noble trombone . . ."

The Tuba

Have you ever stopped a moment to consider that the stuff of which we are made, our bodies themselves, with all their different shapes and sizes, are necessary just to carry us around, just to give us a form? What we *truly* are is something else, something deep within us, something which perhaps is called by those who consider such things more than I, soul.

I don't think much about this sort of thing, but just the same I can never quite forget how big and clumsy I am, how — I suppose I must face it — awkward-looking and even ridiculous I must appear to some people. Can they not see and understand that the music I make is what is really important, that my sounds, which are often deep growls — the deepest in the entire orchestra — and sometimes velvety soft and full of feeling, are really what I am deep down inside? When will they realize that there is something more true and more real than what we can see with the eye or touch with the finger? When will they begin to listen with their hearts?

"When will they begin to listen with their hearts?"

THE PERCUSSION FAMILY

We are placed in the back of the orchestra for a good reason. We are its backbone; we keep the time and the beat, and we also supply the punctuation marks in music – particularly exclamation points! We do not need to be scraped or tickled or blown upon, for our sounds come from being given a good whack – or sometimes just a gentle tap – with a mallet or a hammer, and here we are.

The Triangle

I know that those who listen to music could do without me, for the sound I make is no big thing. And yet, when I do strike my clear and bell-like tone, they hear me, and they know it came at just the right time. True, it is only a single sound, one that never varies, but — ah! — what a glorious one it is, like fine and delicate glass breaking or like a silver bell moved by a breeze on a mountaintop.

I wait and I wait, for my time does not come often, but I am patient. It *will* come, and when it does, I will be ready. Why are they all surprised when they hear a sound which is so much like the tinkle of an icy stream deep in a green forest? They murmur to themselves, and they say to each other, "Did you hear that tiny voice there, just a moment ago? It was lovely, wasn't it?" And then they forget in listening to all my friends. But I will be back, and then they will remember once more.

"I wait and I wait, for my time does not come often."

The Timpani

The only thing really important in life is rhythm; rhythm, beat and timing; everything depends on these. It's all well and good to bring forth grand melodies, and I must admit that they often entrance me, but when it comes down to basics, where would anything be if it weren't for my rhythm-keeping and my booming voice. I can rattle and clatter, too; I can be fast, a blur of sound and of movement, or I can produce just a single, smashing reverberation that always comes, mind you, at precisely the proper moment. I am usually a sort of backdrop, a foundation, and what could be finer than to be so fundamental? To play a glowing melody? Sometimes I think that might be nice — to do that just once, maybe. But I'm not complaining, not really.

"The only thing really important in life is rhythm."

The Cymbals

People look at me and immediately they think, "Crash! Bang! The cymbals again!" But how mistaken they are, for "Crash, Bang!" are such weak words, words better suited to describe the noise of a box falling down a flight of stairs or of a pot smashing on a stone floor. I make music! And when I am needed in the orchestra, it is not to play a melody or to be a background but to explode with a sound like the splitting of a mountain, like the bursting of a rising sun on a tropical morning, like an exultant shout of triumph! It may be a little true that in order to be quite so magnificent I must give up something, something that some of the other instruments have, something that has to do with melodies and softness, but there are all kinds of beauty, aren't there, even the kind which I can produce?

Why is it that I never have a moment to be completely alone, that I am more like an exclamation mark than a complete sentence, that I need the other instruments so much? I *do* have a part in the making of beauty, don't I?

'' 'Crash, Bang' are such weak words!''

The Bass Drum

I don't often wonder too much about anything, but I *do* wonder why it is that so many simple things have to be made so complicated. It seems to me that after one removes the unnecessary frills of things and gets down to basics, everything is really quite simple.

Take me, for example: I don't need miles of tubes, or delicate reeds, or complicated keys, or things that slide or go up and down. All I require is to be clean and reasonably tight, and a simple, sharp blow of a stick — at the right time — will produce a sound which no one can misunderstand or ignore. What more could anyone want? To be understood and to be paid attention to: that is basic, simple, and satisfying.

Why is it, then, that although it is so simply clear that all things are better when reduced to simplicity, there are those who *prefer* to be complicated, difficult to understand, and — as they like to say — subtle? That's a complicated question, and I am not concerned with it. Stand back! Listen! Here comes a sound everyone will be able to understand!

"Stand back! Listen! Here comes a sound everyone will be able to understand!"

INSTRUMENTS WITHOUT FAMILIES

> *We have chosen to be by ourselves,*
> *we want it that way, and here we are.*

The Harp

I don't mind being part of the orchestra, but I really don't think I can ever be *completely* a part of it. For I am in a world of my own, a world of gently flowing waterfalls of sound, a world where harshness and pain do not exist, a world where there is no suffering but only beauty. My tones are golden and always rippling, rippling, as the hands of the harpist caress my strings in soft circles of movement. I don't quite understand why any world must exist other than mine. There must be a reason, but I really can't be concerned about it because my purpose in life is only to create my own special kind of radiance, and that is all I am really concerned about.

"My tones are golden and always rippling, rippling . . ."

The Harpsichord

Clarity and precision are the basic qualities of anything that is worthwhile. It is very bad indeed to cover up a lack of these attributes either with sounds that rattle windowpanes or with those that are so faint they cannot even be heard.

I am precise and I am clear. My strings are plucked, not struck, and the music that is the result is always distinct and exact. I can be played slowly or quickly, and I have a vast range of tones, from high to low, but I see no reason to vary their volume much or to merge one with another any more than is necessary. Now, the piano is my friend, and, in fact, we are related, but I am older, probably wiser, and certainly more precise. I have to smile a little, inwardly, when I hear the piano trying to impress everyone with great romantic oceans of sound. It is the quality, not the quantity, of things that is important, and it is the delicacy of the precisely accurate that is the essence of truth.

I answer all questions truthfully, accurately, and precisely. Would you like to know why music is beautiful, why it moves us to laugh and to weep with joy at the same time, why it gives us a glimpse of the divine? I wish, I do *so* wish, that I could answer those questions clearly and precisely!

à Lloyd Bowers

"I am precise and I am clear."

The Piano

I stand alone. I am the prince! I am the prince of instruments, the prince of music-makers. Loud, soft, fast, slow, happy, sad — I can be and I am all of these and more. I can produce sounds that are like the soft sighs of lovers, the thunderings of storms, the jokes of clowns, the joys of life, the pains of death. I can be shallow, I can be deep, I can be like nature, or I can be as precise and careful as arithmetic. I can be played all alone, or I can be played with the whole orchestra as a background without being overwhelmed. I stand alone in my royal place.

But prince or not, I exist for only one reason, one reason that gives me life and soul. I exist for the sake of music, and while I may be the prince of instruments, music is my king!

"I am the prince!"

A Few More Instruments

So we are put here as a sort of miscellany, are we?! This is a "catch-all" page, is it, because we aren't considered sufficiently important to be given pages to ourselves?! We don't even have a title at the top of the page! Well, never mind! *We* know that we *do* make unique and valuable contributions to the orchestra and that they are important in themselves. Try to eat a steak without salt, potatoes without butter, Mexican tortillas without pepper! Do you see? We add spice to the orchestra, richness to otherwise bland sounds, color to plain little melodies!

We are the xylophone, the tambourine, the chimes, the gong, the snare drum. But we weren't given our own pages, so we aren't going to tell you which is which! Figure it out for yourself!

"We add spice . . ."

PART II

The Final Family

THE CONDUCTOR

Sometimes we come together, joining with the conductor, who combines all our splendid qualities into one perfect whole. Here he is, alone at first, and then as our leader, as the head of the orchestra, the final musical family.

The Conductor

I am the leader, the head, number one. The entire orchestra is my instrument, and I can make it one voice just by the motion of my hands. I move my hands a certain way and it begins, another way and it stops. I induce it to rise and fall like a great tide of sound just by the way I move my hands and my body. I play the orchestra as a puppeteer plays his puppets, and as I smile or frown, beckon or wave away, it moves with me and does my bidding. I give it a soul, and it becomes a living, breathing extension of my will.

But I am kind and indulgent, too. I know that the secret of a good leader is to persuade his followers that they are each important as individuals, even though when *my* followers all come together, it is I, I who make it possible for them to produce the total sound that none can create alone.

What would the music of the symphony be without me? But then, on the other hand, what would *I* be without the instruments which make the music and without the music itself to guide me, to show me what I must do? And where would I be without the artist who composed the music in the first place? Is it possible that I, who control all the instruments, can myself, despite my importance, be controlled by something beyond me? Can it really be that I am not the most important, that I am also in a way an instrument? That is difficult for me to believe, for I am not used to being humble. After all, I am the leader, the head, number one, am I not?

"I am the leader, the head, number one!"

The Orchestra

Here we are together, finally, no longer as individuals or as members of separate families but as parts of one big family.

"I am capable of elevating the soul . . ."

MOZART · TCHAIKOWSKY · ROSSINI · STRA

The Orchestra

I am the orchestra. I have many parts, and they are all important, but I make of them something far superior to what any is by himself. And although each instrument is different and proud to be different, when they all come together, each forgets his individuality and each does his share in the realization of a mightier goal than any can attain alone.

I am the symphony orchestra, and through the guidance of the conductor and under his firm control, I unite all my separate elements into a creation greater than wood, brass, silver, or gold, greater than sounds, greater than the people who compose, than the people who play, than the conductor himself. And although I know that I can never completely escape my earthly limitations and that in the midst of the serious there always lurks a touch of the ridiculous, I know, too, that I can create a sublime kind of beauty unsurpassed by anything in this world. I am capable of elevating the soul to that lofty pinnacle of understanding and feeling where it can reach out and almost touch the outstretched hand of God.

FINIS